D1606617

EXPLORING WORLD CULTURES

El Salvador

Alicia Z. Klepeis

Cavendish
Square

New York

Published in 2020 by Cavendish Square Publishing, LLC
243 5th Avenue, Suite 136, New York, NY 10016

Website: cavendishsq.com

This publication represents the opinions and views of the author based on his or her personal experience, knowledge, and research. The information in this book serves as a general guide only. The author and publisher have used their best efforts in preparing this book and disclaim liability rising directly or indirectly from the use and application of this book.

All websites were available and accurate when this book was sent to press.

Library of Congress Cataloging-in-Publication Data

Title: El Salvador / Alicia Z. Klepeis.
Description: First edition. | New York : Cavendish Square, [2020] | Series: Exploring world cultures | Includes bibliographical references and index. | Audience: Grades 2-5.
Identifiers: LCCN 2019010924 (print) | LCCN 2019011865 (ebook) | ISBN 9781502651679 (ebook) | ISBN 9781502651662 (library bound) | ISBN 9781502651648 (pbk.) | ISBN 9781502651655 (6 pack)
Subjects: LCSH: El Salvador--Juvenile literature.
Classification: LCC F1483.2 (ebook) | LCC F1483.2 .K54 2020 (print) | DDC 972.84--dc23
LC record available at https://lccn.loc.gov/2019010924

Editor: Lauren Miller
Copy Editor: Nathan Heidelberger
Associate Art Director: Alan Sliwinski
Designer: Christina Shults
Production Coordinator: Karol Szymczuk
Photo Research: J8 Media

Printed in the United States of America

Contents

Introduction

El Salvador is a country in Central America. Throughout its history, different groups have ruled what is now El Salvador. Today, it is a free country. Its government is a **democracy**.

El Salvador has beautiful mountains, lakes, and rain forests. Visitors from around the world come to enjoy the country's beaches and colorful villages.

The people of El Salvador are called Salvadorans. Salvadorans have a variety of jobs. Some work in national parks or hotels. Others have jobs in schools or marketplaces. Many Salvadorans grow crops like coffee and sugar.

There are lots of delicious foods to try in El Salvador. The people also enjoy music and art. Sports like soccer and basketball are fun for everyone. Many festivals and celebrations take place during the year.

El Salvador is an amazing country to explore!

People enjoy swimming at El Imposible National Park in western El Salvador.

El Salvador is located in western Central America. Honduras lies to the north and east. Guatemala borders El Salvador to the northwest. The Pacific Ocean is next to El Salvador.

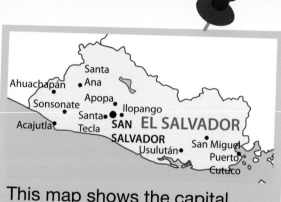

This map shows the capital, San Salvador, and other important cities.

FACT!

El Salvador has a tropical climate. This means it is warm year round, especially along the coast. In the mountains, it's cooler. It's usually rainy in summer and dry in winter.

6

The Land of Volcanoes

El Salvador has many active volcanoes. The last big eruption was in December 2013. There are also frequent earthquakes.

El Salvador covers 8,124 square miles (21,041 square kilometers).

El Salvador's southern coast has flat plains with many farms. There are volcanoes across the rest of the country. Northern El Salvador is also very rocky. The Sierra Madre Mountains are located here.

The country's largest river, the Lempa, runs through northwestern and central El Salvador. Most Salvadorans live in the middle of the country on a high, flat area called a plateau.

7

Ancient people like the Olmec, Maya, Toltec, and Pipil lived in what is now El Salvador. They had large cities and temples.

The Tazumal ruins are a reminder of the ancient Maya.

Spanish explorers came to El Salvador in the 1500s. The country was controlled by Spain until 1821. From 1823 to 1840, El Salvador was part of a **federation** with Honduras, Nicaragua, Guatemala, and Costa Rica. It broke up in 1840. Then, El Salvador became independent.

El Salvador means "The Savior" in Spanish.

Saint Óscar Romero

Óscar Romero was an **archbishop** in the Roman Catholic Church who fought for human rights in El Salvador. He was nominated for a Nobel Peace Prize in 1978.

This is picture of Saint Óscar Romero from 1979.

In the 1850s, Salvadorans began to grow coffee. It brought many jobs. Coffee farmers had lots of power over the government. This caused problems between the rich and the poor. A civil war broke out in 1980. It lasted for twelve years. Today, El Salvador is not a rich nation, but it is a growing one.

Government

Today, El Salvador is a democracy. It has fourteen departments, which are like states. The country's capital is San Salvador.

The government was once based in the National Palace. Today it is a national monument.

El Salvador's government has three parts: legislative, judicial, and executive. The legislative part is called the Legislative Assembly. The members of the Legislative Assembly write new laws. The judicial

FACT!

All Salvadoran citizens over the age of eighteen can vote in elections.

In 2018, twenty-six members of the Legislative Assembly were women. The first female vice president, Ana Vilma de Escobar, was elected in 2004.

former vice president
Ana Vilma de Escobar

part is made up of courts. The courts decide how to apply the laws. They follow the country's constitution. The constitution was adopted in 1983. It describes all the basic laws of El Salvador.

The executive part is made up of the president and the Council of Ministers. The council helps the president run the government.

El Salvador has one of Central America's largest **economies**. It trades with countries like the United States, Honduras, Guatemala, and China. In 2001, the US dollar became the country's money.

A worker picks coffee cherries on a farm in western El Salvador.

Some Salvadorans work in banks, hospitals, and offices. Others have jobs in stores and schools. Farming is important too. Crops like coffee, sugar,

FACT!

More than 2.5 million tourists visited El Salvador from other countries in 2018.

Sending Money Home

Over three million Salvadorans live in other countries. Many of them send some of the money they make back to their families in El Salvador.

women working in a factory in Valle San Andres, El Salvador

beans, and rice are all grown here. Along the coast, people fish for seafood.

Factory workers in El Salvador make many different products. Clothing and furniture are two examples. Salvadoran factories also produce **ethanol**. This liquid is added to gasoline to make vehicles better for the environment.

Many plants and animals live in El Salvador. Coconut and palm trees grow along the southern coast. Grasses, small trees, and bushes cover the central plains. Pine

Montecristo National Park is home to the El Trifinio rain forest.

and oak trees grow in the mountains.

El Salvador has birds like toucans, herons, pelicans, and wild ducks. Armadillos, snakes, and

FACT!

The rain forest of El Trifinio is protected by three countries: Guatemala, El Salvador, and Honduras.

14

Making Electricity Another Way

Electricity is made in different ways. Some electricity comes from waterpower. Wind power and solar power are also becoming more popular in El Salvador.

iguanas live near the coast. Animals like spider monkeys and anteaters live in the forests. Cats like jaguars and ocelots live there too. White-tailed deer live in the central plains.

Many forests in El Salvador have been cut down for firewood and farming. This means animals lose their homes. Getting clean drinking water is also a problem. Many water sources are unsafe because farms and factories **pollute** them.

Over six million people live in El Salvador. Many of them live near the capital city of San Salvador. It is a very crowded city.

A family poses for a photo outside their home in El Angel, a town north of San Salvador.

Around 86 percent of Salvadorans are mestizo. This means they have both Native American and European ancestors. The second-largest group in

The average person in El Salvador can expect to live 75.1 years.

Palestinians in El Salvador

More than one hundred thousand people of Palestinian ancestry live in El Salvador. In February 2019, El Salvador elected a president with Palestinian ancestry named Nayib Bukele.

El Salvador is white people. They make up around 12 percent of the country's population.

Less than 1 percent of Salvadorans are Native Americans. Most have ancestors from the Pipil tribe. These people often live in southwestern El Salvador, near the border with Guatemala. Unfortunately, the native people living in El Salvador are often treated poorly.

In El Salvador, most people live in cities or towns. San Salvador is the country's biggest city. It is home to over one million people.

A man makes corn tortillas at a factory in the town of Suchitoto.

Because there are so many people, there are not enough houses for everyone. Some people live in shacks made of sheet metal and plastic. Many homes have too many people living in them. Crime and gang

FACT!

On average, most Salvadoran families have one or two children.

violence are problems in El Salvador's cities. Wealthy Salvadorans often live outside cities. Their homes have swimming pools and security systems.

In the countryside, Salvadorans work on farms. Homes here are typically made of **adobe**, wood, or concrete blocks. Many do not have electricity or running water. Life is hard. People often walk or travel by pickup trucks or buses.

Women Workers

More women are starting to work outside the home in El Salvador. In 2017, about 41 percent of the country's workers were women.

A woman mixes concrete at a building site in Las Mesitas.

Religion ✝

Religion is important for many Salvadorans. Most people are Christian. They celebrate holidays like Easter and Christmas.

A parade starts off the Festival of El Salvador del Mundo.

The country also has some unique religious celebrations. The Festival of El Salvador del Mundo takes place each August. It celebrates the country's **patron saint**, El Salvador

FACT!

The Cathedral of Santa Ana is a beautiful Catholic church. It was made a national monument in 1995.

National Holidays

Nearly all of El Salvador's national holidays are Christian. In fact, it is one of the only countries to observe Easter for four whole days, from Thursday to Easter Sunday.

The Cathedral of Santa Ana was completed in 1913.

del Mundo (the Savior of the World). There are parades, street parties, and other fun events.

Some Salvadorans do not follow any religion. A very small number of people also practice other religions like Islam, Hinduism, and Buddhism. El Salvador has no official religion. People are free to believe what they want.

Language

Spanish is the language of El Salvador. The government uses Spanish. Businesspeople also use Spanish. Kids in El Salvador have their school lessons in Spanish.

El Boulevard de Los Héroes in San Salvador is a street that has signs in both Spanish and English.

English is the most popular foreign language taught in schools. People also sometimes speak English for work.

Salvadoran Sign Language became a recognized language in 2005.

Caliche

Caliche (ka-LEE-shay) is a kind of Spanish spoken in El Salvador and other parts of Central America. It includes words and phrases from Native American languages.

A small number of Salvadorans still speak Native American languages. Nawat, also known as Pipil, is one example. Unfortunately, this language is in danger of dying out because there are so few speakers. Some communities in El Salvador are teaching this language to children in school to try to save it. The hope is that people will continue to speak Nawat in the future.

Arts and Festivals

Art is important to Salvadorans. The town of Ilobacso is known for pottery, especially *sorpresas*, or surprises. They have colorful, egg-shaped tops. Hidden underneath are figures of people doing daily tasks like working or cooking.

A craftsman works on a ceramic piece in the town of Ilobasco.

At the Festival of Palms and Flowers in Panchimalco, people create beautiful flower arrangements and have parades.

Claribel Alegría

Claribel Alegría was a famous Salvadoran writer. She wrote poetry, books, and stories for children.

Claribel Alegría in May 2017

The town of San Sebastián is known for handmade hammocks and blankets.

There are many styles of music in El Salvador. *Cumbia* is popular. It has a bouncy feel to it. *Chachona* music comes from the eastern part of the country. Bass is an important instrument in this music. People often dance to it.

Salvadorans celebrate their independence from Spain on September 15. There are parades and fireworks.

Salvadorans know how to have fun. They enjoy sports.

Soccer is the most popular sport. Both kids and adults play. People in El Salvador also love watching soccer games in person and on TV. Basketball is another well-liked sport.

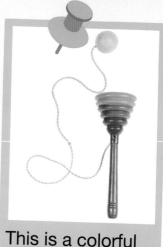

This is a colorful *capirucho*.

FACT!

Estadio Cuscatlán is one of the biggest stadiums in Central America. It is where El Salvador's national soccer team plays home games.

An Ancient Landmark

Thousands of people visit Tazumal every year. This site is home to the most famous Mayan ruins in El Salvador.

A group of children visit the Mayan ruins in Tazumal in 2016.

Salvadorans enjoy spending time outside. Both locals and tourists enjoy hiking in El Salvador's national parks or camping in the mountains. In the waters on the coast, people like surfing and swimming. Fishing is another common activity.

A *capirucho* (kap-ih-ROO-cho) is a traditional toy in El Salvador. Children toss the bell-shaped part of the toy in the air and try to catch it on the handle.

The three most common things in Salvadoran cooking are tortillas, rice, and beans. Most people in El Salvador do not eat much meat. This is because meat is

These women are making *pupusas* to sell at a market in Tecoluca, a city in the department of San Vicente.

expensive. Along the coast, people eat a lot of fish and other seafood. Ceviche is a dish made

FACT!

Salvadorans enjoy desserts. *Semita* is a pastry often filled with pineapple jam.

Drinks in El Salvador

Coffee, soda, and fruit juices are all popular drinks in El Salvador. *Pinol* is a drink made of water mixed with toasted, ground corn.

of marinated raw fish. Salvadorans also enjoy shellfish, such as clams.

   Pupusas (puh-POO-sahs) are a popular street food. They are corn tortillas stuffed with beans, meat, or cheese. People eat them as a snack or even a light meal. Street vendors sell them all over El Salvador.

Glossary

adobe A building material or brick made of earth and straw.

archbishop A high-ranking member of the Catholic Church.

democracy A system of government in which leaders are chosen by the people.

economy The use of money and goods in a country.

ethanol A colorless liquid added to gasoline to reduce pollution from vehicles.

federation A political group that unites smaller groups together, like countries or states.

patron saint A holy person that a church, city, or country is dedicated to.

pollute To make something unsafe or unhealthy with waste made by humans.

Find Out More

Books

Markovics, Joyce. *El Salvador.* Countries We Come

   From. New York, NY: Bearport Publishing, 2015.

Simmons, Walter. *El Salvador.* Exploring Countries.

   Minneapolis, MN: Bellwether Media, 2012.

Website

National Geographic Kids: El Salvador

kids.nationalgeographic.com/explore/countries/el-

salvador/#/el-salvador-oxen.jpg

Video

The Real Beauty of El Salvador

www.youtube.com/watch?v=TSoQUHPNCVs

This video showcases the outdoor activities that are

available in El Salvador.

Index

About the Author

Alicia Z. Klepeis began her career at the National Geographic Society. She is the author of many kids' books, including *Everyday STEM: How Smartphones Work*, *The World's Strangest Foods*, and *Francisco's Kites*. She has never been to El Salvador, but she would love to visit.